造福
淨皂的故事

總策劃 / 靜思書軒

The Wisdom of Cherishing and Sowing Blessings
at the Jing Si Abode (3)
Sowing Blessings: The Story of the Jing Si Soap

小福拿起爸爸新買的手工皂，握在手上剛剛好，看起來很樸實，不過這塊手工皂彷彿有股神奇的力量，讓他有種安心的感覺。

「這塊手工皂叫做『淨皂』，要不要一起去花蓮靜思精舍的淨皂軒，拜訪製作淨皂的師父？」爸爸問。

「要！我要去！」小福開心地回答。

The bar of soap fit perfectly in Xiao-Fu's hand. Xiao-Fu's father had bought it and brought it home, and while the soap looked plain, it was filled with a strange energy that seemed to calm Xiao-Fu.

"This soap is called 'Jing Si Soap,'" Xiao-Fu's father said, "Do you want to visit the Jing Si Soap Workshop in Hualien with me? It's in the Tzu Chi Jing Si Abode, and we can meet the Dharma Masters who make the soap."

"Yes! I want to go!" Xiao-Fu replied happily.

「您好，歡迎回家。」德寋師父說。

「您好，我是小福。請問師父，『淨皂』有什麼含義？」小福有禮貌的問。

「『淨』是清淨無染，『皂』是洗滌除垢。」德寋師父微笑說。「這背後還有個故事喔。」

"Hello, welcome!" Master De Jian said.

"Hi, I'm Xiao-Fu! Could you please tell me what the name of Jing Si Soap means?" Xiao-Fu asked politely.

"Jing Si Soap's name in Chinese starts with the word 'jing,' which means clean. The second word, 'zao,' means soap, and it represents cleanliness," Dharma Master De Jian replied with a smile. "There's also a story behind the soap."

「上人，這是我做的手工皂，請您用用看。」德寋師父恭敬的對著證嚴上人說。

師父依循上人童年記憶中，母親自製手工皂的古早配方：無患子加上米糠，做出第一塊手工皂送給上人，希望上人可以使用最天然的肥皂，這是弟子的一份心意。

"Dharma Master, this is the soap I made by hand; please try it," Dharma Master De Jian said respectfully to Dharma Master Cheng Yen.

Dharma Master De Jian had made the soap based on the old recipe Dharma Master Cheng Yen remembered her own mother using when she was still a child: soapberries mixed with rice bran. She gifted the first bar of soap she made, completely natural and toxin-free, to Dharma Master Cheng Yen, as a student offering her best wishes to her teacher.

有一天，上人對德寋師父說：「上次那塊手工皂天然又好用。我在想，不知道這麼好的東西可以讓更多人用嗎？」於是，將『淨皂』大量生產的想法，在德寋師父的心中慢慢萌芽。

「我們一起來了解『淨皂』的製作過程以及更多的小故事吧。」德寋師父開心的提議。

One day, Dharma Master Cheng Yen said to Dharma Master De Jian, "The soap you gave me was very natural and cleaned very well, even without too many chemicals. Perhaps we could provide this soap to even more people."

These words planted the seed of an idea in Dharma Master De Jian, and she started thinking about producing more Jing Si Soap in larger amounts.

"Let's hear more about how Jing Si Soap is made, and other little stories from its creation," Dharma Master De Jian suggested happily.

『淨皂』大量生產的第一步，就是找空間。

德寋師父在精舍附近找到了一間閒置的鐵皮屋，拿了一張白紙和筆，開始用心規劃廠房內部的動線。廠房的設置逐漸完善，隔間木板、辦公桌椅和置物櫃等，這些家具都是精舍的舊物回收。

The first step to making lots of soap was to find enough room to make it.

Dharma Master De Jian found an empty iron-sheet building near the Jing Si Abode. She picked up a piece of paper and a pencil, and started to plan the layout of the workshop. Soon the workshop was set up with partitions, desks, chairs, and cabinets. All of the items were old furniture from the Abode.

第二步，開始製作。

德賽師父發現，他一天攪拌八個小時，還是打不出手工皂最重要的原料 ——「皂漿」。原來，要大量生產手工皂還需要其他的設備，後來有人出售一臺二手的麵包攪拌機，才打出師父理想中的皂漿。

The second step was to start production.

But Dharma Master De Jian soon found that she couldn't make enough of the soap batter—the most important ingredient in soap—if she only mixed the ingredients by hand. More equipment was needed to make lots of soap. Fortunately, someone sold Dharma Master De Jian a second-hand bread mixer, and she was able to use it to make soap batter.

所有添加在『淨皂』裡面的物質，都是自種、自摘、自曬、自磨，不但沒有化學添加物，更是有機栽種。精舍的藥草園中除了有香草植物，還有各種昆蟲等生物，與萬物眾生共存共生，勤奮的勞動生活，也展現佛家弟子的「一日不做，一日不食」的精神。

All of the other ingredients in the soap came from organic plants that had been grown, harvested, sun-dried, and ground up by hand. No chemical additives. The garden at the Jing Si Abode was filled with many aromatic plants. There were also many wild creatures and insects. This was the perfect example of the spirit of "coexisting with nature," while the Dharma Masters demonstrate the spirit of complete self-reliance, where "a day without work is a day without meals."

　　晾曬場的地上鋪滿了曬乾的香草，志工們將曬乾的香草植物磨成粉，裝在一盆一盆的容器裡，這些香草粉末是要入皂用的。

　　「從種植到採收、晾曬、研磨，全部都是人工採摘製作的，不僅符合綠能的精神，也呼應了『清淨在源頭』的慈濟精神。」德賽師父說。

The sun-drying area was filled with aromatic herbs. Volunteers ground the dried plants into powder and placed them into pots. These would be added to the soap later.

"From planting to harvest, drying, and grounding the plants, we do it all by hand. This is the spirit of 'green energy,' as well as the Tzu Chi spirit of 'purity is at the source,'" Master De Jian said.

「師父，為什麼大家在精舍裡都騎三輪車呢？」小福問。

「三輪車是我們的交通工具，載著各種材料或物品，在不同的廠區裡移動。自己搬、自己運，因為真正的綠能就是人類自己。」德寋師父微笑說。

「我走路上學，我也是小綠能。」小福開心的說。

"Dharma Master, why are all the workers riding tricycles?" Xiao-Fu asked.

"The tricycles are how we get around. They can carry ingredients and tools between different workshop buildings. We move everything ourselves, because the best kind of green energy is doing things ourselves," Master De Jian replied with a smile.

"So I use green energy too when I walk to school!" Xiao-Fu declared happily.

盛夏時日，廠房的溫度高達攝氏三十五度，每位工作人員汗如雨下，臉上的表情卻是無比專注。將各種植物粉末倒入皂液後，不停的攪打皂液，這時背景音樂播放著佛號，佛號與攪拌聲充滿了整個作業空間，彷彿把祝福也注入在皂液中。

In the summer, the temperature in the workshop can reach a sweltering 35°C. But even when every worker is covered in sweat, they are still focused on their work. They pour the plant powders into the soap batter and mix it thoroughly, while Buddhist sutras are played in the background. The sound of the sutras and mixing fill the workshop, and become part of the soap. It is as if the blessings are being mixed into the soap as well.

「請問師父，水車是天氣熱時用來玩水的嗎？」小福天真的問。

「水車不是用來玩水的，是用來冷卻皂漿。因為『淨皂』採用傳統冷製法，需要冷卻的步驟，廠房後面的山溪水正好提供了天然的冷卻系統。」德騫師父微笑解釋。

"What about the water wheel, Dharma Master? Do you play with it when it's hot?" Xiao-Fu asked innocently.

"No, we don't play with the water wheel. It's for cooling the soap batter. The traditional way to make soap has a step for cooling, and the mountain spring behind the workshop is a perfect natural cooling system," Dharma Master De Jian explained.

「好多、好大的木盒喔，這是用來做什麼的？」小福很好奇。

「這是木製的『淨皂』皂模，我們把打好的皂漿灌入這些木盒裡面，等皂液慢慢凝固，淨皂的製作就接近尾聲了。」德騫師父說。

"Wow! There are lots of big wooden boxes! What are these for?" Xiao-Fu asked curiously.

"These are the wooden molds for the soap. We pour the mixed soap batter into the molds and let it set, and then the Jing Si Soap is almost finished," Dharma Master De Jian explained.

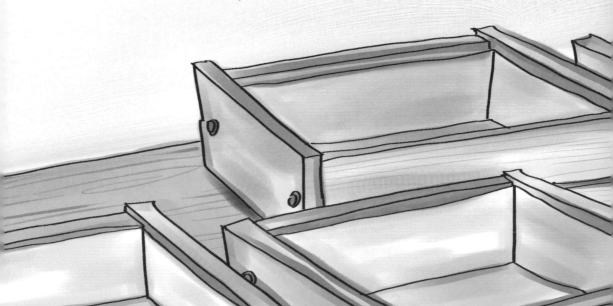

精舍師父和志工們動作迅速的提著一桶桶皂漿，他們將這些皂漿倒入木盒中，這裡需要跟時間賽跑，不然皂漿會慢慢變硬。他們看起來很忙碌，但每個人的臉上始終掛著微笑，神情看起來很寧靜，就像『淨皂』給人那種安穩的感覺一樣。

　　The Dharma Master and volunteers at the Abode picked up buckets of soap batter and quickly poured them into the wooden boxes. They have to move fast, otherwise the soap batter will harden in the buckets. They look busy, but they smile as they work, because the Jing Si Soap gives people a sense of calmness.

皂漿入模之後必須等一段時間，等皂漿凝固、退鹼完成，才可以把淨皂從模型中取出來，這就是一整塊淨皂的樣子。

　　這些『淨皂』的顏色來自於添加的植物粉末，由於沒有任何人工色素，淨皂的顏色是最天然的顏色。

After pouring the soap batter, the workers wait for the batter to set and for the mixture to become less alkaline.

Then they take the big blocks of soap out of the molds.

The color of the soap comes from the plant powders. No artificial colorings are added; all the colors are completely natural.

　　「這是切皂器，把大塊『淨皂』放在這裡，四邊對齊之後，深深吸一口氣之後，再慢慢把線鋸壓下去，就可以把大淨皂切成小淨皂了。切皂沒有祕訣，跟所有作皂的工序一樣，只要專注就可以把事情做好，做任何事都可以抱持這種精神。」德賽師父說。

"This is a soap cutter. We put a big block of soap inside, line up the sides, take a big breath, then push down on the handle. This cuts the big block of soap into small bars. There's no secret to cutting soap; it's just like every other step: just remember to concentrate and do it right," Dharma Master De Jian said.

「咦？『淨皂』不是已經做好了？還要做什麼呢？」小福問。

「上人提醒我們，希望可以將肥皂的邊邊角角修得更加圓潤，可以當成是修改自己的缺點，讓待人處事更加圓融，把出家人的禪意融入其中，也是『淨皂』的一個特色喔。」德寋師父說。

"Oh, I thought the soap was done. What else do we need to do?" Xiao-Fu asked.

"Dharma Master Cheng Yen reminded us that the edges and corners of the soap should be rounded. It represents fixing your flaws and doing things in a well-rounded way. This is what it means to have the Zen spirit, and it's what makes the Jing Si Soap special," Dharma Master De Jian replied.

「以自然農法來種植淨皂所需的原料，將這些植物的能量灌注在淨皂中，每使用一次，都彷彿受到一次大自然的洗禮。

因為不加任何人工成
分的手工皂不香，
不叫『香皂』，但是它可以淨化得很徹底，所以也稱為『淨皂』。」德賽師父下了一個很棒的總結。

Dharma Master De Jian concluded the tour by saying, "Jing Si Soap is made using plants grown naturally, and it is as if the energy of the plants has been infused into the soap. Every time you use it, it's like you're being cleansed by nature. There are no artificial ingredients, and no chemical scents, so the soap does not smell like other soap, but it still cleans very well! This is why we gave it a special name, Jing Si Soap."

「謝謝師父，回家之後，我會更加珍惜這塊『淨皂』。」小福說。

「了解『淨皂』的故事之後，我們要知福、惜福，造福，啟發更多人做更多正能量的事情。」爸爸說。

「我的名字也有個『福』字，謝謝爸爸媽媽幫我取這麼好的名字。」小福說。

"Thank you, Dharma Master, for the tour! I'll treasure this soap even more when I get home," Xiao-Fu said.

"I'm sure that after learning about the Jing Si Soap, you'll spread its message to more people, and will know your blessings, cherish them, and sow more blessings, or 'fu' in Chinese," Xiao-Fu's father said.

"Yes, just like the 'Fu' in my name," Xiao-Fu replied, "Thank you for giving me such a meaningful name!"

製作淨皂的流程
Making Jing Si Soap

淨皂的製作大致可以分成八個步驟，我們一起來了解淨皂的製作流程！
There are eight steps to making Jing Si Soap.
Let's go through them together!

1 種植香草植物
Grow aromatic plants

2 晾曬香草
Sun-dry the plants

5 入皂模
Pour the soap batter into the mold

6 脫皂模
Remove the soap from the mold

③ 將曬乾的香草植物磨成粉
Grind the dried plants
into powder

④ 打皂漿，將香草粉末倒入
Mix the soap batter and
add the plant powder

⑦ 切皂、修皂邊
Cut the soap and round
the edges

⑧ 淨皂完成
The soap is finished

靜思語：造福

以親切的愛心去關懷別人，
這分愛心便是造福的種子。

When we care for others with sincere love,
such a loving heart is a seed of blessing.

《中英對照靜思小語 2》｜《小學生 365 靜思語》

造福人群，就是為自己造福。

In benefiting others,
we in fact also benefit ourselves.

《中英對照靜思小語 4》｜《小學生 365 靜思語》

人要知福、惜福、再造福。

Count your blessings,
cherish them and sow more blessings.

《中英對照靜思小語 1》｜《小學生 365 靜思語》

自造福田，自得福緣。

Those who sow the seeds of blessings shall
harvest plentiful blessings.

《靜思語第一集》｜《小學生 365 靜思語》

有形的物質給別人，無形的福氣給自己。

As we aid others,
we are in fact also sowing blessings for ourselves.

《中英對照靜思小語 4》｜《小學生 365 靜思語》

關於淨皂

給老師和家長們更多關於淨皂的資訊。

東臺灣本地生長，加上純淨豔陽曬乾後的香草，造就純淨因緣。
（攝影者：邱淑絹）

德寋師父與志工一同設計出「手工切皂器」，也成為淨皂軒的特色，不僅讓切皂工作快速有效率，連淨皂的外形也整齊美觀。（攝影者：莊仟垣）

　　有感四大不調日益嚴重，造成人間苦難頻傳，證嚴上人內心甚是憂慮；時為 2007 年，上人不經意地提及現在有許多清潔用品都是化學製品，汙染毒化了土地；而小時候所見生活用品都是純天然製造，例如大人們都是把無患子與米糠曬乾了做成肥皂，引發靜思精舍的師父研發純天然手工皂的因緣。「就是一份堅持，一份無私的大愛，陪伴著淨皂走過一千五百個日子！」「淨斯淨皂」的研發者德寋師父述說一路恆持初心，堅持就地取材，絕不使用化學色素與香料的心路歷程。

　　找時間走訪一趟「靜思書軒」門市，更了解手工淨皂，一起珍護地球資源！

靜 思 人 文
JING SI CULTURE

靜思精舍惜物造福的智慧故事 3

造福：淨皂的故事

總 策 劃／靜思書軒
編　　審／釋德凡
照片提供／慈濟基金會文史處
故　　事／陳佳聖
插　　圖／江長芳
美術設計／陳俐君
英　　譯／ Linguitronics Co., Ltd. 萬象翻譯（股）公司（故事及主題延伸）

總 編 輯／李復民
副總編輯／鄧懿貞
特約主編／陳佳聖
封面設計／ Javick 工作室
專案企劃／蔡孟庭、盤惟心

讀書共和國出版集團 業務平台
總 經 理／李雪麗　　　　　副總經理／李復民
海外業務總監／張鑫峰　　　特販業務總監／陳綺瑩
零售資深經理／郭文弘　　　專案企劃總監／蔡孟庭
印務協理／江域平　　　　　印務主任／李孟儒

出　　版／發光體文化／遠足文化事業股份有限公司
發　　行／遠足文化事業股份有限公司（讀書共和國出版集團）
地　　址／ 231 新北市新店區民權路 108 之 2 號 9 樓
電　　話／（02）2218-1417　　傳真／（02）8667-1065
電子信箱／ service@bookrep.com.tw
網　　址／ www.bookrep.com.tw
郵撥帳號／ 19504465 遠足文化事業股份有限公司

法律顧問／華洋法律事務所　蘇文生律師
印　　製／凱林彩印股份有限公司

慈濟人文出版社
地　　址／臺北市忠孝東路三段二一七巷七弄十九號一樓
電　　話／（02）2898-9888
傳　　真／（02）2898-9889
網　　址／ www.jingsi.org

2024 年 5 月 2 日初版一刷　　　　　定 價／ 320 元
ISBN ／ 978-626-98109-3-2（精裝）　　書 號／ 2IGN1007

國家圖書館出版品預行編目資料

靜思精舍惜物造福的智慧故事 . 3. 造福：淨皂的故事 ＝
The wisdom of cherishing and sowing blessings at the Jing
Si Abode. 3, sowing blessings : the story of soap ／ 陳佳聖
故事 . -- 新北市：遠足文化事業股份有限公司發光體文
化，遠足文化事業股份有限公司，2024.04
40 面；17×23 公分
中英對照
ISBN 978-626-98109-3-2（精裝）

224.515　　　　　　　　　　　　　　113003664